What's for lunch?

Honey

This edition 2003

Franklin Watts
96 Leonard Street
London
EC2A 4XD

Franklin Watts Australia
45-51 Huntley Street
Alexandria
NSW 2015

Editor: Samantha Armstrong
Designer: Kirstie Billingham
Consultant: Godfrey Munro, Park Bee Keeping Supplies
Reading Consultant: Prue Goodwin, Reading and Language
Information Centre, Reading

A CIP catalogue record for this book is available from the British Library
Dewey Decimal Classification Number 638

ISBN: 0 7496 4934 8

Printed in Hong Kong, China

What's for lunch?

Honey

Pam Robson

W
FRANKLIN WATTS
LONDON·SYDNEY

Today we are having honey for lunch.

Honey is a sweet, sticky food.

Lots of people spread honey on their bread.

Eating honey gives you **energy**.

Honey also contains **vitamins** and **minerals** to keep you healthy.

Honey is made by bees.

Bees are **insects** with six legs and four wings.

They make honey and wax,
and **pollinate** our plants and trees.

They make honey from **nectar**
which they collect from flowers.

They eat the honey in winter when there are
no flowers to collect nectar from.

People have always collected honey
from bees in the wild.
Wild bees live in holes in trees
or in gaps under rocks.
Most bees, however, are kept in **hives**
so that people can collect the honey easily.

People who keep bees are called **apiarists**.
They wear special hats and gloves
to protect them against bee stings.
Inside the hives are upright wooden frames.
The bees make wax in their stomachs.
They use the wax to make a **honeycomb**
on each frame.
The honeycomb has hundreds of
six-sided compartments called **cells**.

Every hive has a **queen bee**.
She eats a special, rich food
called **royal jelly**
which makes her large.
Male bees are called **drones**.
They **fertilize** the queen.
The queen lays lots of eggs.
Each egg is laid in one of the cells
in the honeycomb.

Female bees are called **workers**.
They collect nectar from flowers.
They may fly many miles to find it.
When they return they perform a dance
to show the others where the nectar
can be found.

The worker bees store the nectar
inside their stomachs in a **honey sac**.
They pass the nectar to the other bees,
through their mouths.
This turns the nectar into honey.
Then the honey is stored
in the honeycomb cells.
The bees seal the cells with wax
to keep the honey safe.

When the honeycombs are full,
the apiarist pulls them out of the hive
and cuts off the layer of wax.
The honeycombs are placed inside
a machine which spins them very fast
to remove the honey.
Because the bees
no longer have the honeycomb,
they are fed a sugar syrup in the winter.

The honey is **filtered**
and left to stand until
all the bubbles of air
have disappeared.
Now the honey is ready.
Most honey we buy
is a blend of
different kinds of honey.
They are mixed together
in a factory and
then put into jars
or other containers.

A label is put onto every jar
to tell people what kind of honey it is.

The jars of honey are put into boxes
and taken by lorry and ship all over the world.
They are sold in shops and supermarkets.

Honey comes in different colours.
The colour and taste of honey
depend on the nectar
collected by the bees.

Some honey is dark brown and some is light yellow.
Honey made by wild bees in Zambia tastes different from Mexican honey.

Honey was once used
instead of sugar to sweeten food.
It is still used today to sweeten drinks.
It is very soothing to add honey
to a lemon drink when your throat is sore.
You can use honey
to bake a Russian honey cake.

Honey has other uses too.
It can be used in soap
to make your skin soft.
The wax that the bees produce
for the honeycomb can be used
to make candles.
Look how many things we get from bees!

Glossary

apiarist	a person who keeps bees
blend	to mix together different types of honey
cells	the six-sided compartments of a honeycomb
drone bee	a male bee that stays in the hive to mate with, or fertilize, the queen bee
energy	the strength to work and play
fertilize	to start off new life; the drone bee fertilizes the queen. Then the queen bee lays eggs.
filtered	the honey is passed through a mesh or filter to clean it and remove any bits of honeycomb
hive	a wooden structure in which bees live
honeycomb	a wax layer of six-sided cells made by bees. Honey is stored in the honeycomb and the queen bee lays her eggs there
honey sac	a special bag inside the stomach of a bee in which nectar is turned into honey

insect	an animal with three pairs of legs, three parts to its body and usually wings
mineral	something found in honey that helps to build strong bones and muscles
nectar	a sugary liquid made by flowers
pollinate	to carry pollen from one flower to another
queen bee	a large female bee. She is the leader in the hive and the only bee that lays eggs
royal jelly	food fed by worker bees to a queen bee to help her grow large
vitamin	something found in honey and fresh fruit and vegetables that helps us stay healthy
worker bee	a female bee whose job is to collect nectar from flowers

Index

Picture credits: FLPA 6 (T Davidson), 8 (S Maslowski), 9 (David Grewcock), 14 (Silvestris), 15 (T. Davidson), 19 (P. Moulu/Sunset); Holt Studios 7(Nigel Cattlin), 11 (Nigel Cattlin), 12-13 (Nigel Cattlin); NHPA 16 (Stephen Dalton); By kind permission of Rowse Honey, Wallingford, England 20-21 (Steve Shott), 22 (Steve Shott), 23(Steve Shott); Nick Bailey Photography cover, 3, 5. All other photographs Tim Ridley, Wells Street Studio, London.
With thanks to Edward Evans and Jessica Hopf.